Body Work

Body Work

EMILIA NIELSEN

Garry Thomas Morse, Editor

Signature

EDITIONS

Cover design by Doowah Design.
Cover art by Jo Roueche: "Exodus," acrylic on canvas.
Photo of Emilia Nielsen by Rebecca Lippiatt.

This book was printed on Ancient Forest Friendly paper.
Printed and bound in Canada by Marquis Book Printing Inc.

We acknowledge the support of The Canada Council for the Arts and the Manitoba Arts Council for our publishing program.

Library and Archives Canada Cataloguing in Publication

Nielsen, Emilia, 1977-, author
        Body work / Emilia Nielsen.

Poems.
ISBN 978-1-77324-026-8 (softcover)

        I. Title.

PS8627.I42B63 2018   C811'.6   C2018-901290-0

Signature Editions
P.O. Box 206, RPO Corydon, Winnipeg, Manitoba, R3M 3S7
www.signature-editions.com

In memory of
Aase Rita Nedergaard
1926–2000

Body Work

I
Dermographia: (Desire)

Dermographia: (Desire)

a)

More than some accounting of notches, scrapes?
This birthmark, that mole. More than description
(decorative script).
                    To stray, surface. Dig a little.
Become floozy, flimsy: dermographer?*[a]

[i]

Mosquito, fireweed. Whiskey, hairpulling. Biting and lucent.
Skin reeling: meteorshower and thumbtack. Tender, teethmarked:
spit tarnished—

a   Large brain, sweaty body: Human.

*(dermographer): skinwriter. Charts desire's force, skin's text? *Tête-à-tête.* Untrustworthy: doodler, doodling…[b]

b   Why the evolution of hairless skin? Sweat. (Never underestimate the importance of sweating.)

b)

surficial   surgical
not   k(not)
superficial   sacrificial

surface typographical
(but not limited to surface)

necessarily sketchy*

[i]

Salt air, pine. Finding footholds, dive
beneath. Bracing. Breaststroke and tug.ᶜ Undercurrent,
clamber. Rock, warm body. Skin burnished:
sunkissed, burning—

c   Skin, naked and buoyant, reduces drag. This is highly advantageous when swimming.

*(sketchy): skin's evocation. Tricky.
Never the whole _____. Apparition,
(infinitely) pliant. This impressionable
surface—elasticity, restraint. The brain
plastic: gappy, gaper. Keep it together.[d]

d   Functionally naked—literally sweating—when hot, maintain a cool head.

c)

Want skintight. Want floodlight. Watertight.
Want high and dry. Want waterlogged. Hammered.
Want waterproof. Floodgate. Want moonshine.
Want want.

[i]

Expectantskin: blue vein and collarbone.
Unpeeled, articulate. Overfull: _____.

       fracture friction fiction refraction
       resistant resilient refuel
       rapture rupture wrap-it-up

       wretch[e]

e   Why not rest or seek shade? Why become an eccrine machine? A sweating human mess?

[ii]

Electricskin: falter. Rewire, _____.

        refraction a fraction distraction
        ruckus fracas fuckthis
        languor sordid

        wrench[f]

d)

Cityskin, scrawling: asphalt and tar, double
or single yellows, white lines, red. Joined
brick: shit-painted, feathered common (crow,
gull, starling.) Concrete walking path, over-
pass. Turf. Riot of thistle. Razor wire, rat
skid: skunked.

f   For normal brain functioning an even temperature is essential. This is a no-brainer.

[i]

Marked pen-ink tattoo,
ballpoint fly-on-the-wall:
that skin's vernacular of

belt
vein, tedium

        (keep it opaque):
        protest scab-picking

        (keep it raw-boned)*:
        eke it threadbare[g].

g   Eccrine sweat glands have the largest demographic in human skin and secrete copious
amounts of fluid that evaporates quickly during thermal sweats. Fact.

*(raw-boned): desire's skin. Forgo
fastforward impulsion, consumption—
Capitalize on (skin's charming) neediness,
necessity. Improvise: swap and sway[h].

Riff.

h   Sweating skin cools by evaporation. This in turn cools the blood needed by the heart and
     other temperature sensitive organs. Sweat: Think of the cooled blood!

[ii]

(scar tissue): lacks
    skin's elasticity: different,
        laminate: scar tissue
           can't stretch
    move

e)

cicatrisation: decorative scar-
ring, (mark characters); knife-
edge, ink; parse
phrases, tactile
words

dermograffiti*[i]

i   Has no one penned odes, paeans or epigrams to glorious sweat? Someone should.

*(dermograffiti): skin littered, lettered,
lexical. Tagged: solipsistic.[j] Sloppy
pas de deux: medium and meaning.

j   The humble sweat gland is obliged to assume pride of place in human evolution. Take
      that, primates.

[i]

skin = noun (verb):

hide   (cover, conceal)
pelt   (assail, assault, attack)
coat   (smother, spread)

membrane   (shell)
film   (filter)
bark   (peel)

[ii]

skin = verb (noun):

peel   (rind, husk, wrap)
graze   (scratch, scrape)

pare   (skin)

(i)

Need permeability.[k] Superfluity. Need possibility.

k   Even when slightly overheated, thinking, reasoning and communicating are all
     compromised: Brain, you give me fever.

II
Symptomatic

Symptomatic

Tremors

First morning, thought: atmospheric. Unpredictable
uproar, external. Jackhammer roadwork—
too much caffeine? Thought fault line
                             this quaking;
geologic, tumult; thought semi-trailer and traffic.
Thunder, galvanic.[1] Waited, felt chemical.

1   Our skin, a compromise worried over the table of evolution.

Onycholysis

Of finger, nail loosen-
ing from root.   Of
rootless, itinerant. Of
rove, ramble, travel
from nailbed. Of
peripatetic, nomadic.
Of drift and slipping.[m]

m   It's not perfect but does a good job. No matter how hard we wear it, skin remains a fabric
       whose seams won't burst.

Photophobia

Dissimilar to fear, irrational belief,
not the pang of public places just can't.
Can't daylight or fluorescent. Can't sun.[n]
Can't light-filled, luminous. Can't gleam.
Can't glimmer. Can't flash. Can't flume.
Can't bear to. Can't look away.

n   Our skin, a protective shield against the sun. This is to the body's advantage, producing
vitamin D on the spot.

Emotional Lability

Indifferently, indefinitely smashing
plates. Bull in glass house. Gauche,
tactless. Pressed between pages: clinical,
capricious. Performance unremarkable,
unexceptional. Predictable.°

°   Skin is a complex layering of both physical and chemical properties. This laminar
       construction gives the skin its resistance to abrasions and punctures.

Polyphagia

Full: illusive.[p] Bright idea refusing
illumination—conjecture at best—
a failed twenty minute rule; theory
absenting practice, phenomena not
of this appetite, this stomach that begins
and ends, day in and day out—empty
as most questions.

p   It shields us from the environment, resists water, stains, microbes, and many chemicals.
      This outermost layer, the epidermis, is smart stuff.

Myasthenia

Unpredictable, will fervour. Will
force. Will elastic tension.[q] Will
brawn, vigour. Strapping. Will
stature, form, shape. Will
build. Will certainty. Will finale—

q   No matter how we massage our findings, the epidermis will be classified as tough.

Hyperreflexia

Firecracker, when? Kneejerk in a heart-
beat! And how! Fly from socket, out
of joint.ʳ What knocks? What rasps?
What squirrels? What wasps?

ʳ   Probe a bit lower, where a thick layer of dense connective tissue resides. This second
     layer is good to have when in a jam.

Somnolence

Sleep ever present. Sleep: sandwich,
book. Sleep standing and timepiece. Sleep
wild onion and timbre. Sleep cello, brogue.
Sleep wingspan and jog and splendid.[s] Sleep
wink-wink and awkward. Sleep potato and
hum. Sleep soundly, sleep rough. Sleepily.

s   The dermis is made up of both collagen and elastin. Elastin restores normal
      configuration after stretching. And collagen, a ropey protein, holds it all together.

Hypertensive

Ask leapfrog heart to put down
roots, stay put.[t] Roost: seize
time to settle. Settle down, sapper-
ticker. Animal, mineral, vegetable,
blood pumping organ grinder. Heart
on the brain, percussive in throat.

[t]   Our expressive faces convey subtle nuances in relation to what we are feeling. Through
these expressions, we not only have compensated for a lack of tactility via body hair that
can fluff and bristle, some of us can even smile, grimace, or cry on demand.

III
Undone

Undone

What became of taste. The whole fierce being at back of throat? Flame

_____

and how! To be unwound by the stress of corporeality?[u] Dowel, dis-

u   Our skin mediates the tender transactions of our lives.

embodiment.[v] What became of possibility? Maladaptive. Misplaced. What

---

became of excess? Stuck on the leeward side: rain shadow. What became of

v   Skin, at the locus of our information gathering, our relationships with others.

containment, bloated space inside the lines? Hope. What became of flicker-

ing want, phoenixing of quotidian obsession? Snuffed out, self-censored.[w]

w   This continuous covering of the body—skin—safeguards our internal organs from externality.

Then the bottom fell out? Imperceptible drop.[x] And quicksand? Yes! If chased

---

in a corner? Start to swallow that long dragging tail. Waylaid? Infinitely, wind-

x   Far from impervious barrier, the skin is a selectively permeable sheath.

knocked. The sinkhole? Common sense run amok.[y] To become undone, not

---

lost. To double back, unknot and rethread. To return to what never strayed.

y   Works as watchful sentinel, letting some things in and keeping other things out.

Lost: to double back. Unknot and rethread. To return to what never. Strayed,

---

wind.[z] Knocked, the sinkhole: common sense. Run amok, to become. Undone,

z   Skin is more than defense shield, gatekeeper, and personal zoo. Also fact.

not in a corner. Start to swallow. That long dragging tail, waylaid infinitely.[aa]

Then? The bottom fell out: imperceptible. Drop and quicksand, yes. If chased,

[aa]   Pores and nerve endings unite us with our surroundings.

phoenixing of quotidian. Obsession snuffed. Out self! Censored— bloated

---

space inside.[bb] The lines, hope. What became of flickering want? Of excess

bb   Unlike heart or kidney, skin never fails. (It is constantly being renewed.)

stuck on the leeward side? Rain. Shadow, what became of containment?[cc]

Disembodiment, what became of possibility? Maladaptive; misplaced. What,

cc   Our skin imbues us with individuality, forms the vocabulary of personhood.

became and how. To be! Unwound by the stress. Of corporeality: dowel.

What became? Of taste, the whole fierce. Being, at back.[dd] Of throat, flame—

dd   Skin is the interface through which we touch one another and sense future connections.

IV
Done

Done

1.

Now, just past solstice,
a minute of each day drops into night, skipped heartbeat.

2.

Down a no exit lane. Roadside
drifts of cottonwood leaves: yellow,
otherworldly. In a neighbour's pasture
a cross marks something gone. What
do I care? Winter dim, scant
daylight and me impatient.
Get a move on.

3.

Ankles raked a few times. Nothing
that can't be cleaned up with soap,
vitamin E to prevent scars. Give up

stuff easily. Just more to pack.
Changed my last name to no longer
be bound. Before bed, blot the face
with lotion. Complicit in erasure.

4.

Long into an argument
that can't be followed. Imagine
the furnace's fan blade has unwound
from the bolt and whirls loose around the axle.

If it could be stopped, if we could
hold each other for a moment. One leading the other
outside to the deck, stars pressed against the night like bits of flint—

5.

The barking dog in the backyard
hurls herself at a pair of crows.

Charges a bed sheet flapping on the line,
mouths a work glove,
sleeps on the outside doormat
ears pricked for the ticking of a car engine.

Circles the yard,
sky bruises blue.

6.

Cupped in my hands a tough, fragile
thing from a roadside nest of leaves,
still warm and shit-smeared. To take
home, wash, fry in a cast-iron pan.
Delicate blood-scrawl across the albumen—

7.

       At the edge
of the logging road nothing
but tall grass, movement,
a shape out of focus
sharpening—a bear cub
on its hind legs sniffing
the wind. Might have been
standing in a patch of sapling alder
coated in dust, or cottoning fireweed,
fur the softness of seed fluff.
Might have wailed
showing pink gums and milk teeth
as the car cut into morning.
But it faded back into grass
where it first emerged,
fur licked and glowing.

8.

Plump as a stink currant:
tunnelled into belly button,
concealed for hours, ripening
into a small, terrible fruit.

9.

What I bring must fit
the airline's dimensions of checked bags,
anything else I must pay for. It will cost
to take branches, shell, a strand of dried arbutus berry.

Never learned anything the easy way.
Slippage in this transaction: the difference
between estimate and actual.

IV
Undoing

Undoing

(Salt.)

Wind, at midday: when it lets loose over the lake, churlishly. Bad-tempered

(A year later, still caught in current.)[ee]

ee   Human skin: a vast network of nerves and sympathetic nerve fibres.

(Rapture.)

boorish. Not exactly disengaged, but uncoupling. Still tacked on course,
   unwilling

(Dragonfly, eelgrass, driftwood.)[ff]

ff   The sympathetic nervous system can literally save our skin.

(Breath, gravel.)

to redirect; to be moved, by an outcome that can't be transformed. The
    forecast calls

(A path to the bight.)[gg]

gg   Our skin often thinks before we do.

(Flowering grass.)

brass tacks and hammers. Until then, something about star jelly, forks and
spoons. Red

(Belly full of bull kelp and sea lettuce.)[hh]

hh   When nerve fibres in the skin fire, they simultaneously help to constrict the small
arteries in the dermis, activate sweat glands, and stimulate the tiny smooth muscles in
our hair follicles to produce piloerection.

(Cut stem.)

skies at morning. Stormwater and drain. A pint released to gravity. A pot
   unhooked

(Kindling a slow burn.)[ii]

ii   Add dilated pupils: The face of fear.

(Marooned.)

and nothing can undo it, will it back. Pretty much on point. Gravitas: action,
reaction

(Water regularly with dull nails.)[jj]

jj   The cold sweat experienced when nervous is technically referred to as emotional
      sweating. (To distinguish it from thermal sweating.)

(Puncture bubble.)

this feeling, leaves me guessing, grappling. (Except for when it.) After
everything

(A slip, a place between two piers.)[kk]

kk   Flushing in response to anger and blushing in response to embarrassment are fascinating
phenomena, not well understood.

(Gawky itch.)

is said, but not exactly. Losing it. In a singularly fell, unflattering, swoop. Too
    quickly,

(Lifeblood and lifeline: dissimilar.)[ll]

ll   Skin is the largest sexual organ, although we try not to think about it.

(Inking.)

plain and wandering. Wild roses, dusty and dank. Just before dusk. (Before predawn.)

(Cleat and drift.)[mm]

mm   Skin, in subtle and not-so-subtle ways, reflects our existence as sexual beings.

(Pin.)

Sick or unravelling? The sunset: flamingo or conch. You pick. It's your move.

(Unpinning.)[nn]

nn   This sexual flushing of the skin often persists for several minutes, lasting longer than
       blushing. Hot and bothered, as it were.

V
Surgical Notes

Surgical Notes

1[oo]

Send me a button. One

in particular. Blue, missing
from the essential. (Shelter,
regeneration.) Inextricable from

stitched together, skin
hemmed just so.

oo   Many anatomical specializations are responsible for the exquisite tactile sensitivity in
       fingers.

2^{pp}

No visible stitch
no memory of moments
before and after

remains, unreassuringly. Told twice,
three times: better not to remember.
No need to be sheltered from the

unknown. (Some)body remembers.

pp   The skin houses the body's most ancient sense, touch.

3^{qq}

I will stitch the button back to
where absence is clearly marked:

palimpsest. My body dissolves
threading that will remain
untranslated for me. This skin,

matrix-building. This body, that
is—isn't—me, restructuring.

qq   The sensitivity of human fingertips is particularly acute in those who have lost their
     eyesight.

4^{rr}

That I function well without an organ
but don't have the know-how to stitch
a button back in place. Lacking how-to

to do a tidy job. Theatre of incise
and create: divide, separate, divide, mobilize,
divide, identify, identify, divide, separate,
remove, re-approximate, re-approximate,

close up skin with subcuticular stitch.

rr   Touch involves stimulation of the skin by mechanical, thermal, chemical, or electrical
        means. And the resulting sensations of pressure, vibration, temperature, or pain.

5[ss]

This thing, after the fact, of in/completeness,
bio/medically custom/made. And the

quiet drama of remission. (With/out story,
plot points.) Chemically buttoned up.

Necessarily in/complete, purpose-
fully so.

ss   The ends of primate fingers and toes are expanded into large, voluptuous digital pads
that house sensory nerve endings, blood vessels, and sweat glands. And are covered with
fingerprints.

6^{tt}

Sew-thru stitch: thread, knot,
line up button. Push, pull: repeat,
repeat, repeat, repeat, wrap, secure,

cut thread. Fixed? Subcuticular
stitch: throw anchor knot, bite
epidermis, pull, throw, pull, bite,

bite, bite, cinch, cut thread. Variable?

tt   Fingerprints, known also as friction ridges—or dermatoglyphics (literally, finger
writing)—appear on the palms of the hands and soles of the feet of many mammals.

7[uu]

Breach: the body opens. The

quick of hunt-and-peck. Skin
sliced, sutured, dirtied
by cheap sterile marker.

Sequela: I'm off, ever so
definitely un-comely. Feeling
decidedly dis-heroic, un-cyborgly;

try and rub away these. I
need to learn something as vital,
dire as the button stitch.

uu   Different styles of touching abound. (Recall the different kinds of handshakes and hugs
      you've experienced). They are used to send social signals.

8^{vv}

Gown bloodied, feet
bare. (As it were.) How to

embody pain, surrounded by it,
unable to dis/associate from/with it.

Thick and vocal and rank in recovery
room. Vocal and rank and thick in
ward. Rank and thick and vocal:

coda.

vv   Only certain people can touch us this way—like a doctor performing a medical exam.

9^{ww}

I am (not so) self-contained; I am
essentially contained, constrained. Just stop

asking after the subjectivity of feeling; try on
a different question. Call on this volume
of body talk; query skin; seek the subconscious

even because I feel plum. I feel survivalist. I feel
saline. I feel metal and fibre. I feel nexus.

ww   When humans touch other humans, context is everything.

VI
Dermographia: (Repair)

Dermographia: (Repair)

g)

Not a matter of if
but when. Weakest linkage,
the organ most prone, the bone
most tender.

When might it?
When if it?
When?

[i]

Write a new story.[xx] A fresh skin script.
Write the body anew, afresh. Skeins of meaning,
a mess.

xx   Our skin talks even when we don't; it is not a neutral canvas.

> <

You didn't try to kill me only make my life harder.

You try to kill me only, make my life harder.

You didn't kill me, only make life harder.
You try to kill me, make my life harder.

You didn't kill, only make harder.
You try me, make my life.

You didn't only make harder.
You try me, make life.

You only make harder.
You try life.

You make harder.
You try.

You make.
Try.*yy*

Make*.

*(make): poiesis.

yy   It also reflects the heightened human capacity to recognize self in others and to interpret and internalize the complexly coded visual signals that others present to us through their appearance.

h)

Here: embodied, inescapably so. Be a body.^{zz}
Be a skin. Repairing, renewing, rearticulating.

(Was so very.)

Here: relent, relent, slow down. Slacken, supple. Sit still.

Here: tree, deciduous. Huge crows every morning.
So much time spent looking out; skeptical of easy.

Here: bone china, skin thin. Teacup: save nothing
for good. Darn socks, save elastics and green pennies.

(Was busy.)

Here: shatterproof, fragile. Revamp, ever impatiently.

(Was enamoured, so much so.)

Here: whet.

zz   Through the expressive functions of skin and body decoration, we have expanded the communicative potential of our bodies and reinforced the primacy of the visual sense in our sensory repertoire.

i)

allopoiesis: process becoming other,
more than system itself. Becoming umbilical,
branch and star.[aaa] Becoming rot and weft.
Becoming warp and rope. Becoming syntax,
polymer.

aaa   When it comes to our skin—our protective envelope, billboard, and largest sensory
       portal—our scientific and artistic creativity knows few bounds.

[i]

autopoiesis: self-producing, -creating;
living system: more (or less) than machine. Becoming
dialectic: fire and lifeline, ice and leaf. Becoming protein,
organelle, membrane. Becoming mollusc,
cellular.[bbb]

bbb New combinations of practical and aesthetic considerations are likely to yield the most
     surprising changes in human skin-based communication. Changes that will be startling
     in their rapidity and effect.

> <

Second. Guess. Strange. Games. Gotcha. Got game. Keep up. Keep up. Sink.

Flurry. Fast. Fatigue. Faint. Butterfly. Frenetic. Lapse. So.

Protect. Deconstruct. Shape. Choose.

Yield. Shield*. Yen. Yes.

Excess.[ccc] Success. Do dirty. Fight faulty.

Risk. Fumble. Stumble. Stutter. Shallow. Sallow. Iffy.

If. Wait. Farce. Fallow. Irregular. Shadow. Lengthy. Atrophy. Spent. Is. Way much.

(shield): thyroid

[ccc] Ever more sophisticated and interactive virtual reality experiences will become part of our everyday routines, and entertainment based on the interaction of implanted devices with visual and auditory devices in the environment will become commonplace.

[i]

repair = noun (verb)

restoration (return, renewal)
renovation (do up, tart up, tidy up, smarten up)
patch-up (settle, square, resolve)

[ii]

repair = verb (noun)

mend (solution, answer, resolution)
fix (quandary, mess)
seam (ridge, join, closure)

atone (assent)[ddd]

[i]

repair = verb (verb)

recover (salvage, convalesce)
darn (stitch, sew)

recuperate (reprieve)

ddd   The deliciously acute sense of touch that we share with other primates will be
       rediscovered and stimulated in new and unforeseen ways.

[ii]

repair = noun (verb)

haunt (go)

j)

Hear: poplar and hush.
Windbreak and rush.

(Was indefatigable.)

Here: is lake, is loon.
Here: is axe, is melon.

(Was muscle.)

Hear: mosquito and frog.
Vigour and omnivorous.

Here: is wild dog, is wild rose.
Here: is rejoin, is recluse.

[i]

(Was sure.)[eee]

eee   Pressure, temperature, and conductivity sensors implanted under the skin, and in devices
next to the skin, will also radically change the personal sphere of touch.

j)

Here: skin's future, considered. Amorphous,
fraxelated. Retrofit and plucky.

(Scar tissue can move.)*

Here: body's trajectory, reconsidered.
Oddly earthy, myopic.

(Can be coaxed.)^{fff}

Here: pliant, ribbony.

(Can be plied.)

Here: air, fallowing.

i)

(Can become, tangible.)*

fff   Advances in treatments for damaged or diseased skin will be dramatic. But they will be
        overshadowed in the public arena by new ways of enhancing the skin's appearance and
        making it into an ever more dynamic surface for the communication of experience and
        aspiration.

[i]

*(dermapoeisis): skinmaker. Nothing precious or
too pretty: stick and poke. Making skin: crudely
collating, *ad hominem*.[ggg] Epidermis, dermis:
keratin, collagen, elastin. Making, maketh—
cutaneous revision.

[ggg]   Our consciousness of physical appearance and modern society's emphasis on our skin as
a billboard for self-advertisement will only continue to grow.

(i)

*(dermographia): writing skin, (writing repair,
skin repairing), skin writing. Deconstruct
the (natural) dermis, the (natural) shell. Repurpose:

body work, skin talk.[hhh]

hhh   The possibilities are both captivating and frightening and are likely to challenge our
       basic notions of self, physical presence, and personal responsibility.

Acknowledgements

I was in the very beginning stages of this project when I was a part of the summer Poetry Colloquium at Sage Hill and benefited from the insight of mentor Daphne Marlatt and my fellow participants who inspired and challenged my thinking. At the midpoint, the gift of time at Emma Lake as part of the Saskatchewan Writers' Guild Summer Artists and Writers Colony at the University of Saskatchewan's Kenderdine Campus. It was a pleasure to be a part of the Banff Centre's In(ter)ventions: Literary Practice at the Edge and to emerge from this residency with the first full draft of this manuscript. My thanks to each of my fellow participants and, especially, mentor Fred Wah for his support. Without financial support from the Canada Council for the Arts in the form of travel grants I would not have been able to attend these writing residencies.

I'm grateful also to Quest University in Squamish, BC where I was a Postdoctoral Teaching Fellow from 2013–2015. There, I not only had a chance to share this manuscript in progress but also to integrate poetry and poetics as part of my interdisciplinary university teaching. My thanks also to the University of Alberta's Department of Women's and Gender Studies and the Feminist Research Speakers Series—and, especially, organizer Chloë Taylor— for inviting me to present this work as part of a creative-critical talk.

My sincere thanks to Julia Emberley, editor of the special issue on "Skin" of *English Studies in Canada*, for publishing several pages of this poetry in its earlier form. Thank you also to Ally Day and Kim E. Nielsen, editors of *Disability Studies Quarterly*, for publishing my creative-critical paper that integrated several earlier versions of these poems. Thanks also to editors at *The Antigonish Review* and *Event Magazine* for publishing much earlier segments of these poems.

Anita G. Jablonski's *Skin: A Natural History* was exactly the resource I needed when seeking to learn about human skin. In the footnotes throughout my text I have both paraphrased Jablonkski's research as well as repurposed her prose so that phrases of it now stand as bits of found poems.

These poems were written in a period of time that traversed health, illness, solitude and repair. Friendships that could sustain hard conversations were invaluable to me. Thank you for standing by me in the hard years: Maleea Acker, Kris Elder, Elena Johnson, Vivienne McMaster, Alyssum Nielsen, Annika Nielsen, Coco Nielsen, Jo Roueche, and Bren Simmers. Special thanks also to my mum and dad.

Thanks to Garry Thomas Morse for belief in this manuscript and for ensuring it became a book. My thanks also to publisher Karen Haughian and to all the fine folk at Signature Editions. Special thanks to Jo Roueche for the use of her beautiful painting, "Exodus," as cover art for this book.

Finally, my partner Alison Dowsett makes everything that much better. And Pippa Bo ensures we both get up early to write and also get out for frequent walks in the woods—thank you for taking care of us, sweet furry friend.

About the Author

Emilia Nielsen's debut collection of poetry, *Surge Narrows* (Leaf Press, 2013), was a finalist for the League of Canadian Poets' Gerald Lampert Memorial Award. Her poems have appeared in literary journals across Canada including *Descant*, *The Fiddlehead*, *Grain*, and *PRISM international*, which nominated her work for a Pushcart Prize. She holds a PhD in Gender, Race, Sexuality and Social Justice from the University of British Columbia, a MA in English from the University of New Brunswick and a BFA in Writing from the University of Victoria. Throughout 2017–2018, Emilia was a Visiting Scholar at the Canadian Literature Centre at the University of Alberta. In summer 2018, she will join York University as Assistant Professor, Department of Social Science, in the Health & Society Program.